D1560951

WITHDRAWN

UNIVERSITY OF MICHIGAN LIBRARIES

Questioning Cultural Appropriation

Jonita Davis

Enslow Publishing
101 W. 23rd Street
Suite 240
New York, NY 10011
USA

enslow.com

Published in 2019 by Enslow Publishing, LLC.
101 W. 23rd Street, Suite 240, New York, NY 10011

Copyright © 2019 by Enslow Publishing, LLC.

All rights reserved.

No part of this book may be reproduced by any means
without the written permission of the publisher.

Library of Congress Cataloging-in-Publication Data

Names: Davis, Jonita, author.
Title: Questioning cultural appropriation / Jonita Davis.
Description: New York : Enslow Publishing, [2019] | Series: Racial literacy |
Audience: Grade 7–12. | Includes bibliographical references and index.
Identifiers: LCCN 2018020364| ISBN 9781978504684 (library bound) | ISBN
  9781978505636 (pbk.)
Subjects: LCSH: Imitation. | Adaptability (Psychology) | Cultural property.
Classification: LCC BF357 .D38 2018 | DDC 155.2/4—dc23
LC record available at https://lccn.loc.gov/2018020364

Printed in the United States of America

To Our Readers: We have done our best to make sure all website addresses in this book were active and appropriate when we went to press. However, the author and the publisher have no control over and assume no liability for the material available on those websites or on any websites they may link to. Any comments or suggestions can be sent by email to customerservice@enslow.com.

Photo Credits: Cover, p. 1 Pablo Martnez/EyeEm/Getty Images; p. 5 Bloomberg/Getty Images; pp. 6–7 Poras Chaudhary/Stone/Getty Images; p. 8 © iStockphoto.com/talent bender/Getty Images; p. 10 Fabio Diena/Shutterstock.com; p. 12 Boston Globe/ Getty Images; pp. 14, 18–19, 56 © AP Images; pp. 16–17 Jim West/Alamy Stock Photo; p. 23 Igor Dutina/Shutterstock.com; p. 25 David Tran Photo/Shutterstock.com; p. 27 kobbymendez/Shutterstock.com; p. 29 Tono Balaguer/Shutterstock.com; pp. 32–33 Entertainment Pictures/Alamy Stock Photo; pp. 34–35 India Picture/Shutterstock .com; p. 36 Dragon Images/Shutterstock.com; p. 37 Valery Sidelnykov/Shutterstock.com; p. 40 AJP/Shutterstock.com; p. 42 Simon Scott/Moment/Getty Images; p. 44 Giles Clarke /Getty Images; p. 45 mimagephotography/Shutterstock.com; p. 48 Andrey_Popov/ Shutterstock.com; pp. 50–51 Grant Faint/Photolibrary/Getty Images; p. 53 ton koene /Alamy Stock Photo; p. 54 hvostik/Shutterstock.com; p. 58 DigiPub/Moment/Getty Images; p. 60 CJM Grafx/Shutterstock.com; p. 62 AA Images/Alamy Stock Photo; p. 63 Universal History Archive/Universal Images Group/Getty Images; p. 65 Paul Fearn/Alamy Stock Photo; p. 67 Cookie Studio/Shutterstock.com; p. 68 VW Pics/Universal Images Group/Getty Images; cover and interior pages background design Ensuper/Shutterstock .com (colors), Miloje/Shutterstock.com (texture).

CONTENTS

Introduction

In May 2017, two white women—Liz Connelly and Kali Wilgus—opened a burrito cart, Kook's Burritos, in Portland, Oregon.[1] The cart was shut down days later after claims of cultural appropriation. Connelly and Wilgus specialized in tortillas made using the traditional recipe and process of the women of a small village of Puerto Nuevo, Mexico. Connelly told reporters the villagers taught them how to make the tortillas and that they gave the information freely. Despite the protests of their cart, the women didn't think their act was cultural appropriation. It was.

The color run has become a very popular fund-raiser. During the event, runners race while wearing white or light-colored clothing. People line up and throw colorful powders at the racers. The color run was stolen from another culture: Hindus in India celebrate a centuries-old religious holiday called Holi, a celebration of the coming spring.[2] People dance while throwing colorful powders in the air. There are also special foods, drinks, prayers, and more dancing. Holi was stripped down to just color powder and appropriated by American nonprofits and schools.

A woman from a rural Mexican town prepares corn tortillas made by hand at the market.

Color run fund-raising events are watered down versions of the vibrant Holi festival celebrated in India. This picture shows the intensity of not only the color powders but also the participation by all involved.

One well-known case of cultural appropriation happened in 2016, when Kim Kardashian rocked "boxer braids" as her new hairstyle.[3] She took credit for the braids in many pictures and posts before people started calling her out on cultural

appropriation. Turns out, her "new" hairstyle has been worn by several cultures and for centuries. For example, people descended from African tribes have used braiding for sending messages, showing their wealth, and more. Kardashian's case is more obvious, but just as harmful as the color run and the burrito cart.

All three cases are cultural appropriation, despite the different ways it happened. The act of cultural appropriation requires the taking of something that is unique to a group of people. A more dominant culture often does this. Some call it outright stealing. In cases like the Portland burrito cart, the information was not stolen but shared. The problem is that Connelly and Wilgus took the shared cultural information and used it for their own profit. The recipes and lessons were never theirs to make money from.

Taking from another group of people is only one part of cultural appropriation. This doesn't happen with just events, hair, and recipes. As you see with the Holi/color run appropriation, cultural elements can be rituals as well. These can be artifacts, technology, and even processes that are unique to a certain group of people. Cultural appropriation is taking a cultural element from a people and using it out of context or without context at all.[4] It's also something we all have a responsibility to prevent.

This is a cornrow braid style that is typical among black girls, teens, and women. However, the styles are deemed "fashionable" when white celebrities appropriate the cornrow style as a new trend.

American history is full of cases where cultural appropriation was left unchecked and caused harm. It doesn't matter if the cultural item was taken for personal gain, profit, or fame. The outcome is ultimately the same—to harm the minority culture, the one whose things are stolen. The parts of an appropriated culture can get picked off, pulled apart, absorbed, and assimilated until the original culture becomes unrecognizable. Sometimes all that is left is a ghost of the culture in a shell created by the people who took it. In many cases, it looks nothing like the original at all.

CHAPTER 1

Identifying Cultural Appropriation

The one thing that people get hung up on is the "taking" part of cultural appropriation by the dominant culture. That "taking" often ends up damaging the original culture in some way. Taking something from another culture can happen a few different ways. Before you begin going out and questioning cultural appropriation, you must understand all these various pieces.

The Curious Case of Bruno Mars

Bruno Mars has come under fire because of his hit songs that often borrow Black hip-hop, jazz, and blues sounds. Writer Seren Sensei led the charge, claiming that Mars's "racial ambiguity" allowed him to steal from Black culture and profit from it.[1] She went on to say that because he wasn't Black, Mars should not be able to use the music of Black culture as he constructed his songs.

Mars is not racially ambiguous: he is Filipino, Jewish, and Puerto Rican.

Sensei is so concerned about Mars taking from Black culture, she failed to see that the other elements of cultural appropriation are not satisfied. Although Mars is not Black, he also does not come from the white majority, which dominates under American or Western cultural terms. In fact, Mars comes from two cultures that have been heavily assaulted by dominant white American culture. Yes, he is using Black music traditions and combining them with his own to make new sounds. However, because he is not a part of the dominating

Bruno Mars is an artist whose live shows and recorded music sample from African, Caribbean, hip-hop, and R&B, which has caused many Black critics to accuse him of appropriating. For a few reasons, he is not.

culture, technically he is not appropriating. More important is the fact that most white people see Mars as darker skinned and "probably" Black anyway. Thus, in a way he is thrown into the same category as Blackness because of his mixed heritage. This is not damaging to Black culture at all.

One of the reasons we must question cultural appropriation is because that dominant culture will take from others, change it, and use it in a way that can damage the original culture and replace it with a whitewashed version. Mars does make changes to the sound, but he brings more fans to it and shows cultural *appreciation* with songs that hail back to older versions of the sound from the 1980s and 1990s. Sure, he profits from it, but he does not damage hip-hop only to replace the original with a whitewashed copy.

What's Hair Got to Do with It?

The spring of 2017 saw several stories involving Black girls who were being punished for wearing natural hair or braids to school. In Boston, 15-year-old twins Deanna and Mya Cook were suspended for refusing to remove their box braid hairstyle.[2] Meanwhile, the Kardashian sisters grace the pages of fashion magazines and capture headlines in "boxer braids." Rachel Dolezal is a white woman who wears faux "natural" hair to pretend she is Black.[3] Both Kardashian and Dolezal soak up public attention, wearing styles that Black girls and women are chastised and punished for.

This is another very complex side of cultural appropriation. Black girls are expected to assimilate their hair—to damage their hair with chemicals and heat to straighten their

The Cook sisters, Mya (left) and Deanna (right), were disciplined for sporting a style that the Kardashians are praised for.

natural curls. The result is a whitewashed look that, if forced to prevail, will end up wiping out braid and natural styles—except for Kardashian's braids and Dolezal's "curls." Punishment for these hairstyles is also a common problem with cultural appropriation as well: white teens copying the Kardashian look are trendy and fashionable, but on black girls like the Cook twins, it's a punishable offense. This double standard is another way that cultural appropriation damages. Punishing the origin culture forces them to stop or reduce their use of the culture, and theirs is soon replaced by appropriated version.

The Damage Is the Problem

Another issue to consider when questioning cultural appropriation is the damage that can be done to the culture because of the "taking." Set aside Bruno Mars for a second and let's go back to the burrito cart story. The Mexican women who gave the two white women information about their cultural practices was a small group with no money. Not many knew about their tortilla recipe outside of that area in Mexico. The two Portland women had the potential to make the tortilla recipe known throughout the western seaboard if their burrito cart was a hit. They had access to capital (or money) and customers to make this happen. They could have eventually overlapped the Mexican women's area, making "Kook's Burritos" so well known that people even in Mexico wouldn't realize the original recipe came from there.

Some of you may say this is a stretch and a lot of elements must come together to make this happen. Well, let's examine the restaurant chain KFC and its "new" Nashville Hot Chicken.[4] Nashville Hot Chicken was taken from an original recipe that has been sold for decades by Black cooks—the Prince family of Nashville in their family restaurant.

This kind of damage posed by cultural appropriation can be called erasure, since it illustrates the power that cultural appropriation has to overtake another culture's hold on its own proprietary elements. This erases the original culture's link to the element. In the KFC Nashville Hot Chicken case, the Prince family and Black community in Nashville are no longer connected to the dish. Despite the use of the location in the name of the dish, there is no way for KFC customers to

The national appetite for Nashville Hot Chicken is fueled by an American fast food chain's cultural appropriation of a Nashville family's signature dish sold at their locally run diners.

know where the chicken recipe truly comes from. KFC also changed the recipe so that its Nashville Hot Chicken does not taste like the original. All anyone will know is the KFC version. This is erasure.

As the dominant culture takes things, it often does not preserve the origins. Look at the Holi/color run example. Little mention is ever made of Holi on color run fund-raiser sites. The only way you would learn about Holi is if you have a connection to, or knew something of, India and its culture. To millions of people in the United States, color runs were created within the last decade and have no religious connection. See how dominant American culture, because it has so huge an influence, can erase a culture and its practices?

Now imagine what happens when a people are forced or feel the need to assimilate into American culture, or leave their culture behind to take on American habits and traditions. Cultural assimilation is when a dominant culture tries to absorb a minority culture.[5] It often means giving up language, foods, clothing, religion, accessories, and more to survive as well as fit in America—at least on the surface. Slowly, cultural traditions and practices from elsewhere are folded into ours or are erased as the people become more "American." Sure, you could go online and find the origins of the element, like Nashville Hot Chicken, but doing so does not change the minds of the millions buying that chicken from KFC instead of the Prince family. When the Prince family's restaurant shuts down from loss of business to KFC, their original chicken will be gone as well, erased and replaced by the KFC version.

Swallowed in Four Generations

Cultural assimilation can happen as a majority culture absorbs the minority culture because of proximity or the passage of time. Consider immigrant families over generations. The first generation born in America is raised by immigrants, so they know the traditions and language. That first generation intermarries and has children who are bicultural and heavily influenced by the dominant culture. The children are second-generation immigrants and are still connected to their home culture. They probably still have contact with their immigrant grandparents, grow up in a bilingual household, and experience their culture when extended family gets together.

This is harder by the third generation because many people connecting them to their origin culture have passed away. First-generation grandparents may still cling to tradition, but their descendants have been raised in American culture and their handle on the origin culture will not be the same. Some families are fully assimilated by the third generation.[6] Others take until the fourth generation to fully take on American culture. Assimilation in these cases is not

It does not take long for the children of immigrants to assimilate into the dominant culture. Sadly, with every new generation, a part of the origin culture is stripped away.

necessarily forced, but because the family lives in proximity to a dominant culture that can often be racist, bigoted, or prejudiced against foreigners, it can be an easier life in America to adopt more mainstream American culture, like clothing and food.

Think of the slaves from tribes all over the African continent, kidnapped and enslaved in America. They were forced to learn the language, wear the clothing, and adopt the habits of white settler-colonists. These Africans were forced to do so under the threat of death or brutal punishment. However, the slaves were so resilient that they created Black culture from all the pieces and parts of African cultures they were able to keep in secret. These included recipes, braid styles, spiritual songs, and healing methods. Many of these survival-born traditions are still used today. Have you ever been to a Black wedding and seen the couple "jump the broom"? This tradition came from slaves wanting to marry but having to do so in secret. Marriages between slaves was forbidden. Jumping the broom was easy to mask as a dance ritual, something other than the marriage ceremony it stood for. Even this tradition has been appropriated by white couples trying for a "hip" wedding,

but who don't understand the origins. Jumping the broom is the result of forced assimilation, as is so much of Black culture. Black culture, however, is still a fractured history full

"Jumping the broom" is a wedding tradition with roots in slavery, like many other modern African American traditions. It is born from the dominant culture's influence on a minority culture—so that the enslaved could marry without facing often fatal consequences.

of elements that are unknown because so much was lost. The significance of this is that many elements carry the history of slavery and the struggles of Black people throughout history. Like jumping the broom is more than a marriage ritual, many Black cultural elements are flush with the long history of Black people, and they must be preserved.

The emotional weight of the damage to Black culture as a result of America's bloody history of slavery is what leads people like Sensei to become outspoken protectors. However, in the case of Bruno Mars, she is wrong. Mars, despite what some see as his ambiguous heritage, is not from a dominating culture. His use of Black music also does not damage the original. This example shows that to call out appropriation, you must be able to identify what's taken, a dominant culture doing the taking, and damage done because of the taking.

Consider the Bruno Mars scenario if the singer was born to an Irish dad and white American mom. Could you call it appropriation? Discuss.

CHAPTER 2

Appropriating Culture in Food

Google "food near me" and see how many of the restaurants suggested have strictly American food: burgers, fries, hot dogs. If there's a Taco Bell or Pizza Hut, eating there means straddling the lines of cultural appropriation, right? What about Olive Garden's Americanized Italian fare? Got gyros? That's Greek. With food, so much cultural appropriation and assimilation have gone on that it's often difficult to decide if you can eat safely outside your home without participating on some level. Eating in isn't always safe either. Does your family have a Taco Tuesday? Let's discuss cultural appropriation in food and if it's OK to eat anything after this lesson.

Food Is Full of Appropriation

Food is a prominent part of so many cultures, and when these people come to America, they bring their food traditions with them. It's natural to share in the foods of other cultures. In fact, many of the food establishments that are owned by immigrant families benefit from the dollars of adventurous eaters who want to share in their culture's food. So, go ahead and order from that Ethiopian place you love, or grab a bite from that new gyro shack. Doing so is just a way of showing an appreciation for the food and rewarding them with your continued business.

Rachel's Pita Shack

Consider this fictional example: Rachel is a white woman who decides she can make a gyro that isn't as spicy as the one at the gyro shack downtown. She wants a vegan option as well, and she has a great idea for a dessert gyro. She has so many ideas that she opens a gyro shack, but she calls it Rachel's Pita Shop (because everything is on pita bread). Rachel is appropriating Greek as well as Lebanese culture. Despite her intentions to create something "new" from the gyro or to improve upon it, she is still taking a food from Greek culture, changing it, and presenting her version for sale on the same market as the Greek immigrant-run pita shack downtown. This is the cultural appropriation of food.

Rachel's changes sound harmless, but they threaten to erase the original Greek food and distort it by making people think her dessert gyro is authentic. It's not. When white Americans who are known to prefer less spicy food flock to Rachel's place, she is also taking customers from the actual Greek gyro shack, which threatens its livelihood. If it goes under, the only example of Greek food will be Rachel's bland, Americanized gyros. The damage is done, and that

Turkish, Greek, and other Middle Eastern cultures have a pita sandwich of sorts that is often appropriated by American companies. The Westernized versions of the dish often don't come close to the original.

neighborhood or city's original Greek gyro is erased and replaced with Rachel's.

The Problem with Chipotle

Restaurants like Chipotle also work this way to change Mexican food by "improving" on a burrito.[1] The restaurant offers its own build-your-own burrito, using its version of the spices and ingredients Mexican cooks use. The result is a place where customers can walk in and dictate how they want traditional Mexican cuisine constructed. Consumers can bypass the restaurant in town owned and operated by Mexican Americans creating authentic food from their community. Where your local Mexican-owned restaurant will make fresh tortillas daily with corn masa by family recipe and by hand, Chipotle's tortillas are factory-produced en masse for the restaurant. Chipotle's burritos are made faster and with more choices, which has a fast-food appeal to some. Chipotle, like Rachel's Pita Shop, threatens the cultural basis of these foods and disrespects the makers of these foods in their quest to Americanize and capitalize off of other cultures.

Let's look at this another way. Omar comes to school with tortillas in foil and a container that has beans, rice, shredded pork, and other items. The food smells leak from his locker. At lunchtime, people make fun of his weird-smelling food and funny sandwiches as he places the ingredients in the tortillas and eats it. Meanwhile, Susan's mom brings her Chipotle for lunch. She brags about being able to smell it from the office and points out how jealous everyone else probably is. At lunchtime, her whole table clamors for a bite of the burrito bowl that her mother ordered. It has tortillas on the side in a silver wrapper. The bowl is a mix of rice, beans, shredded pork, and toppings. Susan is the talk of the lunchroom, but Omar has to rush through his lunch to escape the ridicule.

Omar's lunch is the authentic food—the very thing Susan's Chipotle lunch appropriated. But his version "stinks," while Susan's makes everyone envious. This is yet another way Chipotle damages a culture. The racist reaction to Omar's meal is the reason why people will choose the appropriated, Americanized version over the original. If you haven't figured

Chipotle's dish is an appropriation of the staples that many Mexican families use to create everyday meals. But like the cornrows on black girls, the same foods from the culture they originated from are considered inferior.

it out yet, cultural appropriation is driven by racism. It is so ingrained in American culture that Susan and her friends can't see that she and Omar are eating the same meal, but *his* is the real deal.

Is a customer participating in cultural appropriation by eating at Chipotle? The answer is yes. The power here is in the money earned. Chipotle curved the process to cut costs and make money, helping the company wield that power with every dollar paid for its food. The same goes for restaurant chains like Taco Bell, Panda Express, and KFC. When you have alternatives, one way to resist cultural appropriation is to buy from the original makers of the food. Give them dollars and appreciation instead of corporations.

New Food Dilemma: The Hand Pie

One area worth noting is new foods. It can be tricky to determine whether a new food is appropriated or not. Sometimes, you may have no clue. However, the moment a person figures out that a new food is another culture's food appropriated by American culture, it must be questioned. An example is the hand pie.

In 2016, recipes for a new type of pastry—a hand pie—were circulating online.[2] The hand pie was a beef or chicken mixture placed on a piece of dough. The dough was folded over and the ends pressed with a fork. This recipe spawned variations, even dessert hand pies. Then, someone saw a picture: the hand pie was identical to the empanada, a food of many Central and South American cultures like Argentina, Brazil, and Colombia. Someone had taken the empanada and called it a new name, not acknowledging that this food has existed for millennia in Hispanic countries. This damage is erasure, since the hand pie recipes were the trending food story with no credit or connection being made to Latin American food or the empanada. Places and people who had never heard of an empanada were now calling it a "hand pie."

Empanadas are a staple dish throughout Latin America. That is why the news of a "new hand pie" recipe in the cooking world was quickly labeled an appropriation of the cultural food.

The Famous (White) Mexican Food Chef

A more complicated case of cultural appropriation comes from professional cooking. Rick Bayless, a television chef who owns a group of restaurants, is always cooking Mexican food.[3] He is not of Mexican heritage but is a white man from Oklahoma. Bayless has a television show about his brand of Mexican cooking that has spawned a line of spices and foods in national grocery store chains. He has, however, done a lot of work to learn the language and customs of Mexico, studying in the country for many years. Bayless claims that his Mexican food empire is an appreciation because he adheres to tradition. Is this cultural appropriation?

The answer is yes. Bayless is a white male, which gives him privileges that Brown chefs don't have. He can tap into American culture in the same way Susan made classmates jealous by having the same meal that Omar is ridiculed for. It's done without the restrictions of racism that often hinder businesspeople of color. Bayless is also selling his "own brand," or style, of Mexican cooking. It may be traditionally Mexican food, but it bears a white man's face and name, and

Gentrification Equals Appropriation

Communities do change as diverse cultures merge. A predominantly Black neighborhood with an infusion of Latinx families can experience a cultural shift, and this is seen in the foods of the area. Because these two are not dominant cultures, they might coexist and have a little overlap. However, when the community is gentrified, or when a poor community is taken over by white people who come in to "improve" the neighborhood to fit their needs and upper-class white families sweep through, they whitewash the restaurants, among other things. Gentrification often goes hand in hand with appropriation in this way, and it doesn't just happen in food.[4]

Bayless has a barbacoa seasoning that turns beef in any American home into the famous Mexican dish. His sauce whitewashes the original barbacoa because he has toned down the vibrant spices of the original dish and substituted flavors to fit the dominant culture's bland palate.

it may be more likely to be bought over authentic products from Mexican companies. So, people going to Bayless's restaurants to appreciate Mexican culture get a version that is not authentic and attempts to replace the real foods. Bayless and his products could become more popular and spread by the power of American culture's marketing and consumption.

There is a difference between appreciating and supporting a culture and appropriating it. Families can try to make the foods at home and even enjoy "Taco Tuesday" if they are appreciating the culture and using ingredients and recipes that do so as well. They can enjoy Indian, Greek, and Mexican takeout, too. Being aware of cultural appropriation just means questioning where the foods come from, who is making and profiting off of them, and questioning the appropriation encountered in the process.

CHAPTER 3

Cultural Appropriation in Fashion—Clothing and Accessories

Clothing is another area where the line between appropriation and appreciation can blur. Everyone has questions at some point in this area. Is that Black Panther costume on a white toddler appropriation? Why are people getting so bent out of shape about my henna tattoo? Why can't I wear a Native American headdress or Indian bindi to a music festival? There is a way to determine what is appropriation when it comes to fashion.

Appropriation Always Tricks or Treats

Halloween is the time when issues of cultural appropriation pop up. Many people dress up without realizing they may be mocking other cultures or taking their cultural elements and damaging that culture. It can get confusing.

For example, white parents wanting to dress their kids as the character Maui from the movie *Moana* found themselves facing cultural appropriation claims.[1] Polynesian people use tattoos as a cultural element, and similar tattoos appear on the character in the movie. However, the costume licensed by Disney did not feature these tattoos, or at least it didn't after the company pulled its 2016 version of the costume. That version had dark skin and tattoos that kids could slip on. Cultural appropriation is taking an element like the spiritual Polynesian tattoos and ethnic heritage that have immense

The Disney animated film Moana *taught many American families that it is possible to play Maui—the favorite role of the film—without trying to appropriate the Polynesian culture's tattoos.*

meaning to Polynesians and making them another prop on a kid's costume. This diminishes the importance of these sacred tattoos, which damages Polynesian culture. It is like wearing blackface, but for children.

Cultural Items Are Not Costume Material

The one important thing to remember when it comes to costumes is to never try to copy an important part of another culture's heritage, religion, or cultural identity. This means the bindi, South Asian forehead jewelry, and henna designs on skin are off limits because they are essential parts of Indian,

Pakistani, Bangladeshi, Nepali, Sri Lankan, and other South Asian cultures. They are not meant to be "fun activities" at a party or part of a costume. They are part of larger rituals and are reduced to meaningless props when American culture appropriates them. As props, they lose their cultural importance, which distorts and eventually erases their original importance.

Sari, Not Sorry

What happens when the intentions of the person are to honor the element, but they actually use it in another way? Does that protect them from cultural appropriation? Let's look at the case of the "protest sari" for answers.

The South Asian wedding traditions are often appropriated by Western culture, despite their religious and ceremonial origins.

The protest sari was created by an American white woman, Stacy Jacobs, who wanted to show her displeasure with the presidency of Donald Trump. For one hundred days, she wore saris to show her solidarity with South Asian people being harmed by Trump's immigration policies. Jacobs stated that the sari prompts questions, which allowed her to share her platform. She chose the sari after visiting India and falling in love with the hand-woven cloths worn by Indian women. Jacobs insists she studied the culture and history of the garment before picking it for her protests.

Despite her attempts to show appreciation for the traditional garment, Jacobs culturally appropriated the sari to draw attention to her protest. The garment was never meant for such use. Jacobs used her privilege as a white American woman to garner attention for herself through the sari for her anti-Trump protest. The irony is that while many applauded Jacobs for her protest saris, South Asian women who choose to wear a sari or other traditional dress can be verbally or physically assaulted, told to go home, or even killed for expressing their culture.

The sari is a wonderous cloth that often draws microaggressions when worn by South Asian women. But on a white woman using it for political protest, it is viewed as revolutionary with adventurous style.

Profiled by Apparel

Another issue with cultural appropriation in fashion is similar to the problem with natural Black hair styles. Middle Eastern and Muslim men are often profiled by their head- and neckwear.[2] This racial and cultural profiling can result in detention, questioning, searches, seizure of property, and denial of entry into the United States. Meanwhile, white men write travel blogs about how great the keffiyeh or shemagh is.[3] They post pictures of these scarves tied turban style or wrapped around their necks— the same ways that may have gotten a Middle Eastern and/or Muslim man detained. That's how cultural appropriation works hand in hand with white dominance, racism, and prejudice.

Scarves worn by Middle Eastern men have been appropriated by hipsters. Yet, men from the origin culture face discrimination when they wear it.

Once again, appreciating a culture differs from appropriating it. White girls wearing cornrows while on vacation in the Caribbean is appropriation, but learning a traditional hula dance from Indigenous peoples in Hawai'i is not. Donning an "Indian Chief" headdress is cultural appropriation, but having your hair braided and face painted to participate in a Native American celebration you've been invited to by a member of the community is not. Wearing a Middle Eastern keffiyeh because it goes with your outfit is cultural appropriation, but donning a hijab to go into the market while on a trip to Dubai is not.

Respect, Don't Appropriate

Respecting a culture may require you to dive into its fashions, but this is done with the intent to participate in the culture without insulting it. You can wear some of the fashions to show your appreciation in certain situations, but it's important to stay away from the things with religious significance or those things that comprise the identity or heritage of another culture's people. Items with deep cultural, social, and religious connections are off limits because their use by outsiders will only insult, distort, or erase that importance.

What other fashion items may have a cultural importance and should be left to the people of that culture?

CHAPTER 4

Appropriating Religious/Spiritual Practices

Religion should be off limits to something like cultural appropriation, but it isn't. Religious practices have been stolen by American and Western cultures for quite some time. Practices like vision quests and yoga were used originally to connect with a culture's deity or spiritualism, but since have become trends for Americans with disposable income. This type of religious cultural appropriation damages another culture by not only stealing, but by also putting down its beliefs, erasing their importance, and turning the ritual into another beauty treatment. For example, vision quests once were used to guide a teen boy into adulthood. Now they are used to help rich women "find themselves" at expensive retreats. The people who once practiced the religion are barred from participating if they wanted to because of the huge price tags these fads often carry.

Yoga in America

A classic case of this type of cultural appropriation is yoga.[1] In America, yoga is an exercise that involves stretching, breathing, and twisting the body in a calm environment. There are variations like "hot yoga," practiced in a 90-degree Fahrenheit room. Yoga in America is often practiced in upscale studios with mostly white women attending with expensive mats, outfits, and gear.

In India, yoga is a Hindu religious practice that is open to everyone. There is usually no charge. Yoga is used in

Yoga in India is practiced by all, in the open, with no restrictions. Western yoga is often a status activity that can be practiced in expensive spaces with accessories that people in the origin culture could never afford.

conjunction with prayer, meditation, and religious study to keep oneself centered and happy, among other things. In India, no special gear or studio is needed. Yoga is practiced outdoors, at home, and in temples, but always with open air moving through the space.

Western yoga is a whitewashed version of a sacred religious practice, taking place inside, with music, and even with extreme heating on during the summer. It strips away the religious and spiritual significance and any other connection to Hindu culture to turn a tidy profit. South Asian women who would like to participate in their culture in America might not be able to afford to attend these classes, or when they do, they experience racism or microaggressions during the class.

Native American Rituals Appropriated, Too

The spa and relaxation trend has appropriated many religious practices to bring Americans with extra money something new to spend it on. Native American rituals that utilize a sweat lodge and vision quest are used along with other special rituals and practices to help a person find spiritual clarity or achieve spiritual growth. Mainstream American culture took those practices and turned them into spa sessions that are stripped of their spiritual connections and the traditions of the people they originate from. One "sweat lodge" in Chicago likens itself to a sauna that allows for groups to get together and relax in an intimate setting.[2] These sessions are very expensive, which exclude many people as well as those who still use the original rituals today.

The actual sweat lodge experience is not as glamorous or sanitized as the Westernized co-opted version. There's dirt, vegetation, smells (from the animal skins), and more.

Culturally appropriated versions of the sweat lodge and vision quest have done a lot of work to erase the idea of the original version. Few people participating in the appropriated steam treatments probably know that many North American tribes still practice the sweat lodge rituals[3] and that vision quests are meant to be a rite of passage for boys around age 11 or 12.[4] White men sitting in a luxury sauna and women meditating to find their purpose in the world are the image that has pushed aside the tradition, making way for a whitewashed version that is more attractive. The idea of a vision quest is thus changed to be a ritual, practiced by any Native tribe, anyone in that tribe, as a means of self-reflection. Notice how far this version is from the true vision quest and sweat lodge practices?

Nothing Is Sacred

What about the practices that have an origin in several religions? Can something be culturally appropriated if it comes from more than one place? To settle this, let's look at the practice of meditation. It is an activity that incorporates breathing, stretching, and focusing on an idea, object, or goal. The issue with meditation is not access, but the use of a sacred practice in a secular manner, oftentimes for profit. The damage here is the cultural appropriation minimizes the importance of the ritual and its significance for the people who believe in it. It's like throwing a Bible on the floor. To Christians, this is an act of disrespect to their religion and means you don't value their beliefs. Appropriating meditation

Of Headdresses and Football Teams

One of the most popular stereotypical depictions of a Native American (never mind that many very distinct tribes fall under the Native American label) is the "Indian Chief." An older brown-skinned man wearing a crown of feathers has been a symbol in US advertising for decades. This image is still the face of many schools, universities, and professional sports teams around the country. This is cultural appropriation. The image of the leader of a Native American tribe is reduced to a cartoon character and is considered a caricature and nothing more. This damages the authority of tribal leaders and erases the original culture by turning it into a stereotype.

Chief Wilton Littlechild, PhD, is not the image of a tribal leader that Western culture has promoted. He is an attorney who works with several government programs to lift up the cause of indigenous Canadians.

Meditation is free and is not exclusive to any religion. The for-profit secular use of the practice is how appropriators blocked access.

from the various religions that use it is like the appropriators tossed it on the floor.

The mindfulness movement has incorporated meditation in many ways. It disrespects a number of religions in the process. The trends in mindfulness and meditation are all about teaching Westerners how to improve themselves by becoming more aware of their bodies and environments. This is done in posh retreats, expensive workshops, and with all types of fad products intended to aid in the meditation process. The problem is the ways in which meditation is practiced—by Hindu, Buddhist, Muslim, and even Christian practitioners—requires no special tools or spaces. Meditation is practiced by everyone who wants to do so, without a fee. During these sessions, meditation is approached as a sacred ritual done without selfish motives attached.

The mindfulness movement cashes in on religious rituals, and in doing so makes them not so sacred to the people appropriating. As with other culturally appropriated religious rituals, connection to the cultures is severed, and it becomes not a sacred religious practice but a trend.

CHAPTER 5

A Duty to Question Appropriation

As citizens of a global community and as fellow human beings, Americans have the obligation to question cultural appropriation as soon as it is revealed. Avoiding new cultural experiences is not the answer. The universal support of other cultures, their foods, fashion, and activities is needed, especially in an increasingly globalized world. It is also important to educate others on the dangers of cultural appropriation. This duty to question means looking for all the characteristics of cultural appropriation before trying a new food, fashion trend, or activity. Failing to do so could result in danger that affects the global community in a number of ways, including erasure, distortion, deprivation, and whitewashing.

"Erasure" Not "Eraser"

One of the most dangerous effects of cultural appropriation is erasure. When an element is taken from one culture and appropriated by another, parts of that origin culture are stripped away. Those parts are replaced by the dominant culture's idea of the element, an idea that can be more connected to the profits it makes than the culture it came from. The origin culture's connection to the element can be erased by the dominant culture's profitable idea. Soon, people either don't connect the original culture with the element or believe the origin culture uses that element in the way that the dominant culture does for profit.

Erasing a culture's connection to an element makes it easy to rewrite the purpose and meaning of that element. For example, making cornrows a new hairstyle erases the centuries of African people using them for status symbols, communication, and accessories.

Distorting the Connection

Another reason to question cultural appropriation is to prevent distortion. Think of the sweat lodge rituals. American culture has taken the practice and stripped it down for luxury, relaxation, and entertainment, distorting the original use into a mainstream and elite practice instead of a sacred Native American one. Unlike Holi and color runs, the connection between Native American tribes and the sweat lodge practice remains. However, unless a person is determined enough to go online to search for the origins of a sweat lodge, the mainstream idea will continue to be of a general sauna treatment. Who performs the sweat lodge practice, how, and why become questions that are answered with a simple search, but are not necessarily made readily available to the culture at large.

Depriving a Culture

Another important reason to question cultural appropriation is that the massive popularity of a thing could deprive a culture from its use. This is especially true after a dominant culture like white American culture has used it up. When something is taken for use by the trendy icons, it can become unavailable to the origin culture.

Consider the case of bluefin tuna and the cultural appropriation of sushi. Popular love of sushi has boomed over the past thirty years, making bluefin tuna—a staple of the dish—an important fish. Prices for the fish rose to extreme heights. In 2013, a sushi restaurant owner named

Kiyoshi Kimura bought a 489-pound fish for $1.3 million![1] At that price, bluefin tuna became the jewel of the sea. Today, its numbers are dwindling so much that the Japanese government heavily regulates who can fish the bluefin, how they can catch it, and when they can fish for it. This

The tuna market grew immensely when Westerners discovered sushi. This caused overfishing and competition for the traditional fishermen in Japan.

will conserve the fish, although Western demand for sushi rages on.

The problem is, sushi is a food the Japanese have been eating for centuries. Generations of families used to fish for bluefin tuna in the traditional boats and using a pole and  fishing line. The fishermen were called the ippon-zuri.[2] They took some of the catch home to prepare and were able to sell the rest to help provide for their families. Today, however, the licensing required to catch the restricted fish is very expensive. Even then, the ippon-zuri are competing over a much smaller population of fish with people who have no care for the culture but are after the million-dollar tuna. No traditional fishermen can compete with this. Many have given up their businesses and moved on.

Cultural appropriation deprived the ippon-zuri of a job that many families have held for generations. The profits off the tuna made it the target of Western fishermen with more advanced resources. The bluefin was overfished because Western cultures took the Japanese dish sushi and made it a trendy food. In doing so, they drastically increased the demand for the sushi. Commercial fishermen came in with nets, traps, baited lines, and tech that wiped out the population. In the end, Japanese culture is being deprived of a practice (fishing tuna) and a delicacy (the tuna).

Accidental Cultural Appropriation

Unintentional cultural appropriation can occur when appreciation of a culture turns into appropriation. This happens when someone takes part in a culture and ends up trying to honor it in their own way. That "way" becomes profits, and the person has gone from appreciating to appropriating.

Here's a fictional example of unintentional cultural appropriation: Christy, a white woman, goes to an Indian wedding and falls in love with the bride's henna designs on her hands and feet. She loves them so much that she takes a trip to India to study the practice and the artists who make these henna designs. She begins talking about Indian culture and doing henna "tattoos" for her family and friends. They encourage her to get a booth at the local craft fair, where she only charges enough to cover the henna and supplies. Christy is unintentionally appropriating Indian culture when she opens shop and does "henna tattoos" at the fair. The fact that she calls her business "henna tattoos" is another example of cultural whitewashing, since these are not tattoos at all. Christy's booth takes business away from Indian or other South Asian henna. She is unaware of this until someone points out her cultural blunder. She promptly shuts down the booth.

Hazards of Whitewashing

Think about what happens if the elements of a culture are taken and appropriated by white American culture. What happens when every part of the culture has been appropriated? What was that culture once like? What were their practices and traditions? Like the elusive Black culture

Many Western sushi restaurants try to recreate the look of a Japanese sushi bar, but the damage to the culture from their appropriation is done to the tuna population and the livelihood of the ippon-zuri community.

we discussed in the beginning of this book, all these different cultural signifiers meld together until no one knows what the origins were. Black culture maintained a kind of identity, but some cultures that are appropriated by larger American culture can't wring their traditions back, like some Native groups who have been forced to assimilate and leave behind their traditional practices. Cultural appropriation risks that everything ends up looking the same—whitewashed and bland of all the spice and flavor that other cultures bring. Think of it like McDonald's buying out all the other stores until it is the only fast food available. That's the end game of whitewashing. It sucks in all diversity until there is none left.

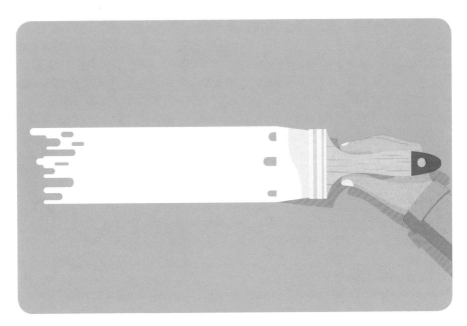

Whitewashing means covering all of the parts that make the element unique to the origin culture.

This is why you must question cultural appropriation. The damage done to the minority and/or origin cultures is often problematic and ends in whitewashing. Questioning cultural appropriation is the first step in stopping the process of cultural erasure. Then, there can be a discussion on how to support and show appreciation for another culture without taking over its practices.

CHAPTER 6

Challenging Cultural Appropriation

There are a few ways to challenge cultural appropriation. American students, especially, have powerful tools they can use to shut down a case of cultural appropriation as soon as it's detected. Cultural appropriation is challenged all the time through social media, protests, and even reporting it to the culture it was stolen from. These are easy for a person of any age to do.

Remember the Portland women and their burritos? They were put out of business by protests that started as soon as word got out about the origin of the tortilla recipe. The protests disrupted the customer service and profits the women expected from selling their food. They had to shut down.

That's the goal of challenging cultural appropriation—to get in the way of the profits or fame the person or company receives from the cultural elements they took. When the appropriator has to pay for the element, it is no longer something they look forward to taking over. This is why informing the origin culture works as well as protests. The Navajo Nation found this out when they were informed that Urban Outfitters was using their name and artwork on underwear it was selling. The tribe came together and sued the retail chain in 2012. They won the suit in 2016 and got the clothes removed from the shelves.[1]

The Navajo designs on women's underwear is offensive. The appropriating culture did not respect the Navajo or their traditional art.

The Power of Social Media

Social media is being wielded as the most powerful place to call out cultural appropriators. All it takes is a news story, video, or post with a picture of the appropriation happening to start things off. Add a few trending hashtags and the call-out goes viral. Soon, people are boycotting, writing to companies, and exposing sponsorships in order to get the appropriation shut down.

A high-end New York restaurant had a dish called fried pork skin. The video blogger who exposed it calls it a chicharrón. It is not surprising that the blogger used the word "chicharrón," since the fried pork skin was the same dish that has existed in Mexican culture for centuries. A chicharrón is fried in seasoned oil and served as a part of a meal. The "improvement" shown in the video was to fry the pork skin in unseasoned oil and serve it with a special dipping sauce. This is cultural appropriation. The video has gone viral sparking a debate on social media. These things usually end in the dish being taken off the menu.[2]

But simply sharing or retweeting these stories is not enough. There are other ways to help end cultural appropriation like the chicharrón described above. Writing a letter or email to the restaurant and/or magazine that printed the blogger's story is a start. Alerting the media is also effective. Publications targeting Latinx audiences would dig into the story to find all the details and report the appropriation to their readers. Once this happens, action occurs. But these causes often need bodies. So, go to the protests, participate in the boycotts, send the emails.

A reworked traditional chicharrón is the newest trend in the cultural appropriation of food.

Everyone has a duty to challenge the appropriation once it's revealed.

People sometimes get too eager about questioning and don't stop to get a good understanding of the situation before the challenge part starts. Remember that cultural appropriation only occurs between two or more cultures where one is more dominant than the other. Revisit the case of Bruno Mars if you need to understand why this happens.

Appropriation involves not only taking from another culture, but also changing and presenting that stolen thing as something new or different for the dominant culture to enjoy. This is true even if the person doing the appropriating researched the culture and calls their products an act of appreciation. Recall the case of Rick Bayless and his Mexican restaurant. The element is not being created by the origin culture, and the racist tendencies of a dominant culture would result in more of the "appreciator's" products being bought. Meanwhile, the people from the origin culture who are cooking the food in their own restaurants could lose sales. The final thing to look for when questioning cultural appropriation is damage to the origin culture or its people. Think back to Omar and Susan, the ippon-zuri, or the Cook twins. Look for ways that the origin culture is losing out to the appropriated version and is being harmed in the process.

The most important takeaway is that standing up and speaking out against cultural appropriation is needed. Don't wait for someone else to do it because they may not have the knowledge to recognize the appropriation. Anyway, why wait for someone else? One person is all it took to start the

The goal of calling out cultural appropriation is to drive business away from the appropriators and into the hands of the origin cultures.

Navajo on their way to court, spark a protest about burritos, and make an upscale chicharrón video go viral. One person who is a part of the dominant culture has a lot of power, and they can help people who are fending off appropriators at every turn. If that one person stands up to challenge the appropriation, other voices will join in.

CHAPTER 7

A Story of Army Blankets and Appropriation

This chapter is designed to test knowledge about cultural appropriation. The following is a fictionalized account based on the true story of the Navajo Long Walk in the 1860s. They were moved from their ancestral land and had to use whatever they could find to survive. The Navajo are resourceful and were able to not only survive, but do so with an artistry the world covets. At select points throughout the story, there are places to pause, reflect, and answer the questions presented. Discuss those answers with a partner or the whole class. Then, continue the story. Let's see how much you learned about cultural appropriation.

Taking Blankets

One winter, several generations ago, a small group of soldiers from the US Army was dispatched to move a

Native American tribe to a reservation. The tribe had been damaged by war. Most of the men were dead or injured. The women ran the tribe. They gathered what belongings they could, and with the soldiers' help, started off to their new home.

They walked for days before hitting a heavy winter storm. The soldiers knew of an abandoned army fort. They directed the tribe there. The plan was to sit out the storm and start on the journey again later in the day. The storm lasted two days, however, locking everyone in. It took two more days to dig a path away from the fort. While they were waiting, the tribeswomen assessed their blankets and clothing. Some needed new clothes, and others needed extra layers

Indigenous cultures like the Navajo were here long before Western culture took over. They can teach us a lot about ancient history if we can help them survive cultural appropriation.

to get through the cold walk ahead. They used the last of their supplies to patch clothing and blankets, but for the new creations, they used what they could find in the base. A surprise stock of army blankets formed the base of their clothes and blankets.

The tribe was known for their colorful blankets and intricate designs. The found army blankets made for a blander selection, but one of the women tried a new form of weaving to incorporate some of the tattered pieces of army blankets from the storeroom. This blanket was warmer and prettier. The rest of the tribe adopted her design.

One of the traditional ways to weave blankets is to build a loom outdoors that's big enough for the finished product.

Has cultural appropriation taken place? If so, who is doing the taking, and what is being taken?

The tribe continued on to the reservation after the storm. They gifted the soldiers with blankets for bringing them safely to the reservation. A kind of partnership had developed. The soldiers took the blankets home to the military base that was nearby. They gave the blankets to their families. The general at the base was so impressed by the tribe's act that he sent a supply of plain army blankets to the tribeswomen. "If you make the blankets," he told them, "I will see that they are sold on base and in the nearby town. I'll make sure the tribe gets all the profits from the blankets."

This arrangement worked for the tribe. They hadn't settled into the new place, so they had no crops, no game from hunts, and nothing to trade for the things they needed. Having money from the blankets would keep them fed through the rest of the winter and into the spring, when they could plant crops and start hunting and gathering their food.

Did appropriation take place here? What do you think of the army general encouraging the tribe to keep the new design that incorporates the army blankets?

This relationship lasted for several generations, and the women passed the army blanket design and business down to their children. The relationship between the tribe and the army continued long after the general moved to another post. The tribe paid the army a small fee for the blankets and a small percentage of their sales. The base and nearby town had grown so big that hundreds of thousands of people lived in the area. The blankets had become not just the tribe's

The designs that the tribes used in their weaving were exclusive to that tribe. Like the Navajo designs on this blanket, the designs in a tribal blanket were distinct.

specialty, but a local favorite. They even had a few shops in town dedicated to the blankets and other items the growing tribe created. The shops were run by a man called Steve, who saw the blankets, loved them, and struck a deal with the tribe to set up the shops and sell them.

Is there some cultural appropriation going on now? Is the army guilty? What about the man who's running the shops for the tribe? If they aren't appropriating, what is really going on?

Today, Hannah goes looking for the tribe with a blanket that is made of a really old design. Someone recognizes it as one of the blankets made before the tribe moved from their original home many years ago. They tell Hannah that only a tribesman would have such a blanket. She goes back to her family to ask questions. She also takes a DNA test. Hannah finds out that she belongs to the tribe. The owner of the blanket was an ancestor who escaped and passed for a white person in a nearby town. She went back to the tribe to live among them and learn their ways.

The Navajo women of that tribe taught Hannah everything, including how to make the blankets. However, she was more interested in the old style of blanket that her ancestor owned. Hannah got some help from the women and learned to recreate that design on a traditional loom. She asked to have one made, which the tribe did, and brought it back home when she left.

After several months, Hannah returned with a check for the tribe. She told them how she wove blankets from that old style and sold them for a lot of money. They took a few dollars to cover supplies and some of her labor, but

Western culture consumes items without consideration for where they came from. This is one of the reasons cultural appropriation is so damaging.

gave most of the money to the tribe. Hannah was selling the blankets on her website.

Is Hannah culturally appropriating? Does her affiliation with the tribe and the financial arrangement change the answer? Does the tribe's willingness to take part in these activities matter?

Hannah's business takes off unexpectedly. She is thrust into the spotlight and into the fashion world. Hannah's new company makes designs inspired by the tribe. Her women's and kid's clothing lines are a hit. She makes a deal to sell at big-box stores all over the country. Her blanket line is

The commercial manufacturing of a cultural element is another form of whitewashing. The designs are simplified, and the intricacies of the origin culture are removed to facilitate mass production.

still operational. The profits still go to the tribe. This is why Hannah thinks her success from using her heritage is OK. She is giving back to the tribe and crediting them with the origin of the design.

That makes her business OK, right? Or is she guilty of cultural appropriation?

The Point

Now that the idea of cultural appropriation has been learned and tested, it is time to go out and do your duty. Keep watch for cases of cultural appropriation. Don't be afraid to question and challenge them. Doing so is the way you can help preserve cultures that struggle to have a voice.

Chapter Notes

Introduction

1. Carolina Moreno, "Portland Burrito Cart Closes After Owners Are Accused of Cultural Appropriation," *Huffington Post,* May 27, 2017, https://www.huffingtonpost.com/entry/portland-burrito-cart-closes-after-owners-are-accused-of-cultural-appropriation_us_5926ef7ee4b062f96a348181
2. "Dyeing Culture: Color Run, Whitewashing Holi Since 2012," *Brown Girl Magazine,* April 2, 2013, https://www.browngirlmagazine.com/2013/04/color-run-controversy
3. Britni Danielle, "Hairstyle Is Not Called 'Boxer Braids' and Kim Kardashian Didn't Make It Popular," *Teen Vogue,* March 17, 2016, https://www.teenvogue.com/story/boxer-braids-hairstyle-history
4. "Cultural Appropriation," *Cambridge Dictionary,* March 5, 2018, https://dictionary.cambridge.org/us/dictionary/english/cultural-appropriation

Chapter 1
Identifying Cultural Appropriation

1. Papa Longlegs, "Seren Sensei Goes Off on Bruno Mars Claims He Stealing Black Culture. Is Bruno an Culture Vulture?," *YouTube,* March 9, 2018, https://www.youtube.com/watch?v=UDflHjSFqZI
2. Crystal Tate, "Why the Two Black Sisters Punished for Wearing Braids at School Is Beyond Wrong," May 15, 2017, https://www.essence.com/hair/Black-sisters-punished-wearing-braids
3. Allison Samuels, "Rachel Dolezal's True Lies," *Vanity Fair,* July 19, 2015, https://www.vanityfair.com/news/2015/07/rachel-dolezal-new-interview-pictures-exclusive
4. Gabe Bullard, "KFC Brings the (Cultural) Heat with New Nashville Hot Chicken," *National Geographic,* January 22, 2016, http://theplate.nationalgeographic.com/2016/01/22/kfc-brings-the-cultural-heat-with-new-nashville-hot-chicken

5. Ran Abramitzky, "What History Tells Us About Assimilation of Immigrants," Stanford Institute for Economic Policy Research, April 12, 2017, https://publicpolicy.stanford.edu/news/what-history-tells-us-about-assimilation-immigrants

6. Susan K. Brown and Frank D. Bean, "Assimilation Models, Old and New: Explaining a Long-Term Process," Migrations Policy Institute, October 1, 2006, https://www.migrationpolicy.org/article/assimilation-models-old-and-new-explaining-long-term-process

Chapter 2
Appropriating Culture in Food

1. Jarune Uwujaren, "The Difference Between Cultural Exchange and Cultural Appropriation," *Everyday Feminism,* September 30, 2013, https://everydayfeminism.com/2013/09/cultural-exchange-and-cultural-appropriation

2. "Rhubarb Baked Empanada," Kevin Is Cooking, August 4, 2016, https://keviniscooking.com/rhubarb-baked-empanadas

3. Maria Goody, "When Chefs Become Famous Cooking Other Cultures' Food," *The Salt,* NPR, March 22, 2017, https://www.npr.org/sections/thesalt/2016/03/22/471309991/when-chefs-become-famous-cooking-other-cultures-food

4. Blights Out, "The Cultural Ramifications of Gentrification in New Orleans," *Shelterforce,* August 23, 2017, https://shelterforce.org/2017/08/23/cultural-ramifications-gentrification-new-orleans

Chapter 3
Cultural Appropriation in Fashion— Clothing and Accessories

1. Carla Herreria, "Disney Pulled that Offensive 'Moana' Costume. Here's Why It Matters," *Huffington Post,* September 21, 2016, https://

www.huffingtonpost.com/entry/disney-maui-costume-brownface_us_57e0c4cde4b08cb14097b892

2. William Hamilton, "Group Four: You've Been Profiled," *Central View,* November 29, 2010, http://www.central-view.com/past.asp?number=1504

3. Matthew Karsten, "Shemagh (Keffiyeh) Scarf: Why I Travel with One," *Expert Vagabond,* November 21, 2017, https://expertvagabond.com/shemagh-keffiyeh

Chapter 4
Appropriating Religious/Spiritual Practices

1. Manasvini, "Ask a Hindu Indian: Is Yoga Cultural Appropriation?," *Medium,* November 24, 2015, https://futuretravel.today/ask-a-hindu-indian-is-yoga-cultural-appropriation-560c7a54f793

2. "Home, Sweat, Home," *Urban Daddy*, March 2, 2010, https://www.urbandaddy.com/articles/9163/chicago/chicago-sweatlodge-home-sweat-home-winter-relief-russian-style

3. Adrienne K, "Sweat Lodges Part II: No You Can't. Here's Why," *Native Appropriations,* April 15, 2010, http://nativeappropriations.com/2010/04/sweat-lodges-part-ii-no-you-cant-heres-why.html

4. "Native American Religion Lakota Indian: Vision Quest," *The Wild West*, accessed April 2018, http://www.thewildwest.org/nativeamericans/nativeamericanreligion/103-lakotaindiansthevisionquest

Chapter 5
A Duty to Question Appropriation

1. Svati Kirsten Narula, "Sushinomic: How Bluefin Tuna Became a Million-Dollar Fish," *Atlantic,* January 5, 2014, https://www.theatlantic.com/international/archive/2014/01/sushinomics-how- bluefin-tuna-became-a-million-dollar-fish/282826

2. Justin McCurry, "Still Hooked: Time Runs Out for Japan's Dangerous Obsession with the Bluefin," *Guardian,* November 17, 2008, https://www.theguardian.com/environment/2008/nov/18/fishing-japan-conservation-tuna

Chapter 6

Challenging Cultural Appropriation

1. Nicky Woolf, "Urban Outfitters Settles with Navajo Nation After Illegally Using Tribe's Name," *Guardian,* November 18, 2016, https://www.theguardian.com/us-news/2016/nov/18/urban-outfitters-navajo-nation-settlement
2. "This Fried Pork Skin Is Reaching New Heights," *Food Insider,* Twitter, April 5, 2018, https://twitter.com/InsiderFood/status/981841375443456000

Glossary

ambiguous When the identity, origin, or definition is unclear or has more than one possibility.

assimilation Taking on the traits of the dominant group in order to fit in. This occurs in immigrant cultures when they settle in the United States.

authentic The most genuine version available. The original or made from the original materials and by the origin culture.

blackface The practice of painting a white person's face black. Its origins are in racist depictions of Black people, so the practice is deemed racist.

chastise To scold a person or express a sharp disappointment in that person.

cultural appropriation When the dominant culture takes the elements of a smaller culture and changes it to be used as a new thing for its people.

culture The customs and traditions that are distinct for a group of people.

deity The god or higher power that is worshiped and/or prayed to.

deprivation The state of taking something that people need away so they no longer have access.

disposable income The wages left after taxes, insurance, expenses, and bills have been paid.

distortion The act of misleading people to believe that one culture owns an element when it actually belongs to another.

dominant Relating to the larger and more powerful people or group.

element The ritual, food, accessory, clothing, or other item that a culture produces. The items are exclusive to that culture.

erasure   The act of slowly removing parts of something until it is all gone, but doing so in a way that is barely noticed.

extinction   Being wiped out of existence.

minority   The less populous and less powerful person or group.

religious practice   The ritual and/or activity that people do when worshipping their deity.

Western culture   The powerful and influential group of developed countries whose values, choices, and practices inform the rest of the world. This culture is predominantly white and includes Europeans and Americans.

Further Reading

Books

Bruchac, Joseph. *Our Stories Remember: American Indian History, Culture and Values through Storytelling*. Golden, CO: Fulcrum, 2003.

Christerson, Brad, et.al. *Growing Up in America: The Power of Race in the Lives of Teens*. Palo Alto, CA: Stanford University Press, 2010.

Dimalene, Cherie. *The Marrow Thieves*. Markham, ON: Dancing Cat Books (DCB)/Cormorant, 2017.

Hayes, Chris.. *A Colony in a Nation*. New York, NY: W. W. Norton & Company, 2017.

Nelson, Kadir. *Heart and Soul: The Story of America and African Americans*. New York, NY: Balzer + Bray / HarperCollins, 2011.

Websites

Beyond the Buckskin
www.beyondbuckskin.com

Cultural Respect
www.nih.gov/institutes-nih/nih-office-director/office-communications-public-liaison/clear-communication/cultural-respect

Decolonizing Yoga
www.decolonizingyoga.com

Groundwork for Change
www.groundworkforchange.org/cultural-appropriation.html

Index

About the Author

Jonita Davis is a writer who studied composition and criticism at Purdue University. She has been writing content and ghostwriting for twelve years, making the change to writing about race, culture, and identity issues after earning her master's in English literature and criticism. Her work has appeared in the *Washington Post*, *People's World*, *Women Under Siege,* and many other publications. She is a contributing entertainment writer and critic on film and television for Black Girl Nerds as well. She has written two other nonfiction books, *Michigan City Marinas* (History Press, 2009) and *Michigan City's Washington Park* (History Press, 2011).

$26.45

LONGWOOD PUBLIC LIBRARY
800 Middle Country Road
Middle Island, NY 11953
(631) 924-6400
longwoodlibrary.org

LIBRARY HOURS

Monday-Friday	9:30 a.m. - 9:00 p.m.
Saturday	9:30 a.m. - 5:00 p.m.
Sunday (Sept-June)	1:00 p.m. - 5:00 p.m.